America's Prairies

America's Prairies

A Carolrhoda Earth Watch Book

written and photographed by Frank Staub

Carolrhoda Books, Inc./Minneapolis

For Linda and Rich

LIBRARY OF CONGRESS CATALOGING-IN-PUBLICATION DATA

Staub, Frank J.
   America's prairies / by Frank Staub.
      p.   cm.
   "A Carolrhoda earth watch book."
   Includes index.
   Summary: Describes the ecology and biology
of the three different types of North American
prairie—tallgrass, mixed-grass, and shortgrass.
   ISBN 0-87614-781-3
   1. Prairies—North America—Juvenile literature.
2. Prairie ecology—North America—Juvenile
literature. [1. Prairies. 2. Prairie ecology.
3. Ecology.] I. Title.
QH102.S73   1994
574.5'2643'097—dc20   93-7841
                                                  CIP
                                                   AC

Manufactured in the United States of America

1 2 3 4 5 6 – I/JR – 99 98 97 96 95 94

"As far as the eye could see in every direction there was neither tree, nor house, nor shed visible...so that we were rolling as it were on the bosom of a new Atlantic...but that sea was of rich green grass and flowers instead of the briny bottomless deep."

So said James Silk Buckingham, an Englishman traveling across the middle of North America in 1837. In those days, this part of the continent was a land of grass with few trees. When the wind blew, all the grasstops moved as one, like a wave on the surface of a great sea. Strange creatures, such as giant bison and burrowing owls, lived there. This was America's prairie.

Any large grassy area can be called a prairie. But technically, the word refers to the vast expanse of grasses that once covered a fifth of North America, from Indiana to the Rocky Mountains and from Texas to central Canada.

Although the kind of grass may vary, all grasslands look pretty much the same. The large grasslands of Asia are called steppes. In South America they are the pampas. The African savanna is a grassland with scattered trees. North America has half a dozen different kinds of grasslands, including desert grasslands, the California grasslands, eastern grasslands, and grasslands in mountainous areas. But the prairie is America's largest grassland.

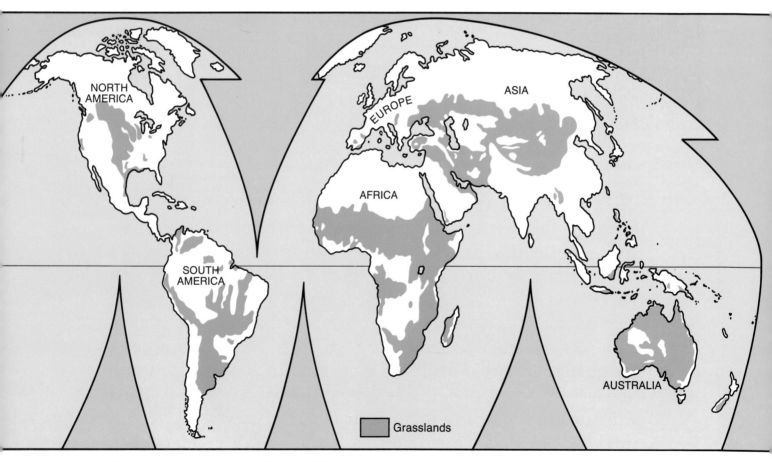

Some of the major grasslands of the world

To the first white settlers who arrived there, the prairie looked unsuitable for farming.

For hundreds of years, a small number of Native Americans lived on the prairie. Although they hunted animals for food and clothing, their impact on the land was small.

The white people who crossed the prairie during the early 1800s didn't change the land much either. They were on their way to California and Oregon. These were mostly farming families from the woodlands of Europe and the eastern United States. Experience told them that to plant crops you had to first cut down trees. This new land of big skies, thick grass, and no forests struck them as harsh and unproductive, not suited for farming. They referred to much of it as "The Great American Desert."

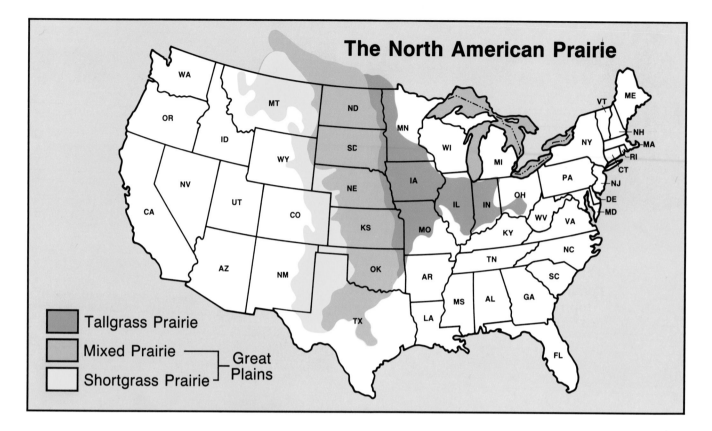

The North American Prairie

Tallgrass Prairie
Mixed Prairie ⎤
Shortgrass Prairie ⎦ Great Plains

As the first pioneers made their way west through Ohio and Indiana, they encountered more and more open, grassy areas. The first prairie grass they saw was tall, incredibly tall, ten feet high in some places. It was so high that cowboys sometimes had trouble finding their cows in it. By the time the early settlers reached the Mississippi River, the land was mostly treeless, and the few trees they did see were clustered in the moist areas between the hills.

As the pioneers headed farther west, the landscape changed even more. Now there were fewer and fewer saddle-high grasses and more and more grasses that were only waist-high.

Farther west the grass was shorter still. Short grass dominated the landscape until the wagon trains reached the foot of the Rocky Mountains.

The three types of North American prairie: *tallgrass* (left), *mixed-grass* (top right), *and shortgrass* (bottom right)

The experience and observations of the pioneers match the system scientists use to classify wild prairie. They divide the North American prairie into three geographic regions based on grass height: the tallgrass prairie to the east (containing grasses over 5 feet, or 1.5 m, high), the shortgrass prairie in the west (less than 2 feet, or .6 m), and the mixed-grass prairie in between. The mixed prairie is a combination of tall grasses, short grasses, and medium-sized grasses (2 to 4 feet, or .6 to .8 m). Together, the mixed and shortgrass prairie make up the Great Plains of central North America. The Great Plains are often called the High Plains because of their elevation, thousands of feet above sea level. Denver, Colorado, which lies along the boundary where the High Plains meet the Rockies, is over a mile above sea level. By contrast, Indianapolis, Indiana, near the eastern edge of the tallgrass region, is only 710 feet (213 m) above sea level.

Storm clouds gather above the tallgrass prairie in southern Missouri. More rain falls on the tallgrass prairie than on the other prairie regions.

As the pioneers left the tallgrass prairie and crossed the Great Plains, they noticed other changes besides a decrease in grass height. The wind blew more strongly and more frequently. Streams and ponds became increasingly rare, and it rained less often. On average, 25 to 39 inches (64–99 cm) of rain fall on the tallgrass prairie each year, while the shortgrass prairie receives a scant 14 inches (36 cm) or less.

Less rain means less moisture. And decreasing soil moisture is why grass height decreases from east to west. In general, the taller a grass is, the more water it needs. The shortest grasses on the western plains are able to survive long **droughts,** or periods when little or no rain falls.

THE WIND BRINGS THE RAIN

Westerly winds help carry enough moisture to the eastern prairie to allow tall grasses and some trees to grow.

In North America, the wind generally comes from the west. These **prevailing winds** are called the westerlies. Before the westerlies reach North America, they pick up moisture from the Pacific Ocean. Later, as they cross the Rocky Mountains, they drop most of this moisture as rain and snow. But by the time the westerlies blow down onto the plains east of the Rockies, they are dry and bring only enough rain to support short and midsize grasses. The Great Plains are thus said to be in the **rain shadow** of the Rocky Mountains. As the westerlies continue eastward, they take on moisture that blows down from Canada and up from the Gulf of Mexico. This increases the rainfall, allowing taller grasses to survive. The farther east the westerlies travel, the more moisture they take on, and the higher the grasses become.

Droughts are caused by low rainfall, but in the Midwest, a high rate of **evaporation** can make them worse. When dry air comes into contact with a moist surface, such as a leaf, a flower, or an animal's tongue, water will leave that surface through the process of evaporation. Water evaporates faster in warm weather than in cooler weather. So the rate of evaporation is greater on the warm plains of Texas, for example, than it is on the cooler prairies of central Canada.

High winds also increase the evaporation rate, and the prairie is a very windy place. The prairie winds are at their fiercest on the Great Plains because there are so few trees and buildings to block the moisture-sucking gusts.

This cornfield replaced native mixed prairie in Minnesota. Inset: *A restored farmhouse near South Dakota*

As some of the pioneers began to settle on the prairie instead of continuing westward, they found that the prairie earth was well suited to agriculture. Farmers were accustomed to growing food crops such as wheat and corn, which are grasses that have been **adapted** for human use. They flourish in the same conditions as wild grasses do. So the pioneers plowed up most of the native grasses and wildflowers and replaced them with crops. They turned cattle and sheep loose to graze on the rest of the prairie land.

For the United States, the vast, food-producing prairies were settled at the perfect time. The country's population was growing rapidly and needed to be fed. However, unlike the small bands of Native Americans who found food on the prairie for a thousand years without having much effect on the land, the great numbers of white settlers almost completely changed the prairie in less than a century.

One reason the prairie is such a good food producer is that most grasses and grass seeds make an excellent diet for many large animals. Another reason is the soil. Grassland soil, especially that of the tallgrass prairie, is soft and full of nutrients that are necessary for the plants' survival. Soft, nutrient-rich soils such as those typically found on grasslands are called **mollisols.**

Nutrients are released into the soil by bacteria and other tiny organisms. These organisms help to decompose, or break down, dead plants and animals by eating them. The decomposers then release the minerals and other substances of which the plants and animals were made back into the soil. The minerals become the nutrients used by new plants.

Grass is a good food source for many animals, including deer.

Early-season forbs on the tallgrass prairie in southwestern Missouri

In addition to grasses, prairie soil is suitable for other plants called **forbs.** A forb is any plant that is not shaped like a grass and is not woody like a bush or tree. The leaves of forbs are wider than those of grasses. But like grasses, prairie forbs are capable of surviving drought. Both the grasses and the forbs of the prairie have very long roots that absorb plenty of water.

The most abundant examples of prairie forbs are wildflowers. It isn't hard to spot them amid the green grasses of spring and summer. Their bright colors attract insects seeking the sweet liquid nectar at the base of each blossom.

When an insect enters a flower to reach the nectar, it comes into contact with **pollen** grains, produced by the male organs of the flower. The pollen sticks to the insect's body and rubs off on the female organs of other flowers that the insect visits. A sperm from a pollen grain then combines with an egg in the female organ to produce new flowers. This process is called **pollination.** Without insects to transfer pollen, many forbs would not be able to reproduce.

Grasses reproduce too. But unlike the insect-pollinated forbs, grass plants are wind-pollinated. The wind transports pollen from one grass plant to another. Grass flowers lack the large, showy petals that characterize forbs. The lightweight pollen grains are exposed to any breeze that might carry them away. This makes it very easy for grasses to reproduce, which helps explain why grass covers a quarter of the earth's surface.

A windswept landscape covered with tall grasses and flowers is an inspiring sight. But early travelers didn't always think so. The thick, high grass on the eastern prairies slowed their wagons and tired their horses. Cordgrass was the most troublesome for the tallgrass pioneers. Also known as ripgut because of the hooklike barbs lining its leaves, cordgrass grows up to 10 feet (3 m) high in thick patches.

Still another name for cordgrass is slough grass, because it thrives in the wet areas around sloughs. Sloughs are muddy areas often found near streams or ponds. They develop in the low places called bottomlands that lie between the prairie hills.

The bottomlands receive the water that drains down from the hills and ridges known as uplands. Trees that grow on a natural prairie, such as the cottonwood and the Osage orange, are usually limited to the bottomlands because of the extra moisture there.

Cordgrass was a challenge to early farmers on the tallgrass prairie.

Much of the original tallgrass prairie, including this section in Illinois, has been replaced with corn.

The broad areas between the sloughs and uplands are neither wet nor dry. On the tallgrass prairie, these areas are dominated by big bluestem and Indian grass. The golden plumes of Indian grass and the colorful stems of big bluestem once covered millions of acres in America's heartland. But the rich soil supporting big bluestem and Indian grass was just right for another tall grass—corn. By the end of the nineteenth century, virtually all of our native tallgrass prairie had been planted in corn. Less than one percent of the original tallgrass prairie still remains. Many people now refer to this part of the country as the corn belt.

Sod is so dense that prairie settlers used it to build houses.

The dark earth underlying most of the tallgrass prairie, as well as parts of the mixed prairie, is anchored by a thick network of roots. Tallgrass prairie forbs and grasses have enormous root systems. The interlocking plant roots combine with the soil to form a dense material called **sod**.

Sod has many advantages over ordinary soil. With so many roots holding it together, the dirt won't blow away during a windstorm. And water doesn't evaporate from sod nearly as quickly as it does from ordinary soil.

Some grasses, such as big bluestem, form sod more easily than others. These grasses are called sod-formers. Grass plants that don't form sod grow in clumps or bunches. Bunch grasses, such as little bluestem, tend to live in drier soil than sod-formers.

"Sod-busting" was a difficult task for the first Midwestern farmers and their horses. The cast-iron plows they brought from the East could barely cut through the dense tangle of roots. Also, the sticky prairie earth clung to their plow blades. Every few steps, a farmer had to stop his team of horses and scrape the plow clean.

In 1837 John Deere of Illinois invented a steel plow that cut easily through prairie sod. More important, the soil didn't stick to its highly polished blade surface. If not for the John Deere plow, the mixed and tallgrass prairies would not have been farmed so quickly.

Restored plows, originally used by pioneers, at the John Deere Historic Site in Grand Detour, Illinois

When the Midwest was covered with sod, trees had a hard time taking root. But today there are many more trees in the prairie states than before, partly because most of the sod has been removed. More moisture is also available for trees because of the amount of water used for crops and lawns. Another reason for the increased tree growth is that fires are no longer widespread on the prairie.

Before the prairie was farmed, scientists believe, lightning caused fires every 3 to 4 years in a given area. The flames would move quickly, burning the dry grass-tops and forbs but leaving their roots unharmed and ready to send up new shoots the following spring. Any trees that had managed to gain a foothold in the sod were burned also. But unlike grasses and forbs, most trees can't sprout new growth from their roots, and so they died.

Prairie fires usually don't do extensive damage to wildlife. They do kill some animals such as snakes and grass-dwelling insects. But many creatures simply leave the burn area. Some find refuge in the moist bottomlands. Others go underground until the flames pass.

Prairie fires were terrifying for the early settlers. But fire has always played a vital role in the prairie's ecology. Like decomposer organisms, fire is one of nature's recyclers. It breaks down the bodies of dead plants and animals and releases nutrients into the soil. Fires also clear away old grass shoots, allowing the new growth to receive more sunlight.

Top: *As the Midwest was settled, the presence of farms, towns, and roads kept prairie fires from spreading. In places where the prairie has been preserved, humans take the place of lightning by starting small, controlled burns.* Bottom: *A section of prairie after a controlled burn. Note the unburned low areas, which were too moist to burn.*

As nutrient recyclers, prairie fires are even more important on the mixed prairie than they are on the tallgrass prairie. That's because decomposer organisms need moisture to break down the bodies of dead plants and animals. The tallgrass prairie has plenty of moisture for the decomposers to do their job. But the mixed prairie does not, and so fire helps do the work of decomposing.

Some grasses grow on both the tallgrass and mixed prairie. Little bluestem, a common native grass of the tallgrass prairie uplands, is the dominant plant of most parts of the mixed prairie. Unlike its tall cousin big bluestem, little bluestem stands no higher than three feet. Also in contrast to the sod-forming big bluestem, little bluestem generally grows in bunches. Side oats grama grass also grows on the mixed prairie, as well as on the tallgrass prairie.

Little bluestem (in background) grows abundantly on this section of mixed prairie in South Dakota.

A hayfield near Dix, Nebraska. Hay is a common mixed prairie crop.

Mixed in with little bluestem on the mixed prairie are blue grama and buffalo grass, the dominant plants of the shortgrass prairie farther west. Other grasses found on a natural mixed prairie are western wheatgrass, Junegrass, and needlegrass. Hillsides sheltered from the wind may support stands of shining sumac and other shrubs. In the bottomlands, big bluestem and even a few trees such as cottonwoods find the moisture they need. No wonder it's called the mixed prairie.

While corn is a moisture-loving tall grass, wheat is a more drought-tolerant midsize grass. And while the tallgrass prairie became the nation's corn belt, the drier mixed prairie became known as the wheat belt. Hay, sunflowers, sugar beets and flax can also tolerate the drier mixed-prairie soil.

Crop irrigation on the shortgrass prairie in western Nebraska

Farther west, on the shortgrass prairie, the soil is so dry that even the bottomlands are often treeless. Here, getting enough water is a critical concern of every living thing. Crops cannot be grown in the near-desert conditions of the shortgrass prairie without expensive **irrigation**—pumping water in from another location such as a river, a lake, or from underground.

Blue grama and buffalo grass grow abundantly on the shortgrass prairie without irrigation. Their root systems are extremely long, so they are able to draw in plenty of moisture from the soil. In addition, the leaves of these grasses are very short. Short leaves have less surface area, and this cuts down on water loss through evaporation.

Both blue grama and buffalo grass are excellent food sources for cattle and other grazing animals. This food source and the lack of soil moisture are the main reasons that the shortgrass prairie is used mostly for grazing livestock instead of raising crops.

Desert plants, such as cacti and yuccas, also live on the shortgrass prairie. During the drought of the 1930s, cactus patches grew so large that, according to one source, cattle had trouble finding a place to lie down.

Prickly-pear cactus (inset) *and yucca thrive in the dry soil of the shortgrass prairie.*

Cattle are now the most abundant grazing animals on the shortgrass prairie. But some native grazers, such as deer, are still common throughout all three prairie regions. Deer do well on the prairie because there's plenty for them to eat, and because they can usually find at least a few trees for protection at night or during a storm.

In spite of some overgrazing by cattle, many of the wild grasses that existed when bison roamed free still live on the shortgrass prairie. This isn't true of the tallgrass and mixed prairies, where most of the native plants have been replaced by crops. Another reason the shortgrass prairie is closer to its natural state than the tallgrass and mixed prairies is that fewer people live there. The western plains from Canada to New Mexico contain far fewer roads, houses, and towns than the grasslands and forests to the east.

A katydid, one of about 3,000 kinds of insects that dwell among the prairie grasses, on big bluestem

An ornate box turtle on the tallgrass prairie

Fire occurs less often on the shortgrass prairie than on the other two types of prairie because there isn't much that will burn. The short grasses offer little fuel. In some ways, grazing takes the place of fire on the shortgrass prairie. Most grazers eat only leaves and stems; just as fire does, they leave the roots unharmed, so plants are able to grow back. Furthermore, the animals' droppings put nutrients back into the soil just as fire does.

Some animals are found throughout all three types of prairie, including some reptiles. Box turtles crawl on the prairie floor, and many different species of snakes slide through the thick grass. Like other prairie animals, these reptiles survive on the prairie because they can hide in the prairie grass or use burrows in the earth to escape **predators**, or animals that hunt them.

27

Two typical prairie creatures—a burrowing owl (top) *and a jackrabbit* (bottom)

Many of the animals in the tallgrass prairie also live in forests. But farther west, on the mixed and shortgrass prairies, we find the true creatures of the plains, such as jackrabbits, prairie dogs, and pronghorn. These species rarely venture east into the tallgrass prairie, where running is difficult and spotting enemies almost impossible.

Certain traits distinguish plains animals from forest dwellers. The creatures of the shortgrass and mixed prairies have adapted, or changed, in order to survive on the open plains. With almost no trees and bushes to block their view, they often have excellent eyesight. And since there are so few places on the open prairie to hide from predators, some prairie creatures, such as burrowing owls, escape by going underground. Burrowing also offers protection from winter cold and summer heat.

Other prairie animals simply run away from danger. Roadrunners, prairie chickens, and other prairie birds can walk better than they can fly. Even the kit fox, which lives on the prairie, is sometimes known as the swift fox. One of the most famous prairie runners is the jackrabbit. Its high-speed escapes are made possible by its long, powerful hind legs.

Plains animals also tend to spend a lot of time in groups. This may be a safety measure. If one member of the group sees a predator getting too close, it can warn the others before the predator attacks. Prairie birds flock together more often than birds in the forest. In the same way, prairie dogs dig their burrows close to each other in sizable "towns."

Prairie dogs at their burrows in a "town"

A prairie dog is not a dog but a small squirrel-like rodent. Early settlers spoke of prairie dog towns covering thousands of square miles. Prairie dogs are thought to have numbered in the hundreds of millions.

Farmers regard prairie dogs as pests because they burrow into fields and destroy crops. Ranchers don't like them either because livestock sometimes break their legs stumbling into the entrance holes to prairie dog burrows. So farmers and ranchers began to eliminate prairie dogs from most of their native homes. Today, these wonderful little creatures are seldom seen outside of parks and other protected areas.

Not all the burrows in a prairie dog town are occupied by prairie dogs. Rattlesnakes hibernate in abandoned tunnels, and burrowing owls nest in them. The black-footed ferret, a relative of the weasel, not only nests in the towns but also hunts the prairie dogs.

As the prairie dog population declined, the animals that depended on it disappeared also. In fact, black-footed ferrets are now so rare that some scientists who study them have never even seen one in the wild. The fate of these prairie animals serves as one more example of how humans have changed the prairie environment in a very short time.

The most famous prairie animals, American bison (sometimes called buffalo), gathered in vast herds during migration. Bison were once found among the tall grasses to the east. But they reached their greatest numbers on the High Plains. At an average weight of 800 to 2,000 pounds (360–900 kg), bison are the largest land animals in North America.

Bison have a special relationship with the much smaller prairie dog. They like to wallow in the soft mounds of dirt around the prairie dog burrow entrance holes. Yet despite the damage they cause to burrows, bison actually help prairie dogs. They keep the grass short, allowing the rodents to quickly spot danger. When the bison move on, their wallows are often taken over by buffalo grass, one of the prairie dogs' favorite foods.

An American bison

A herd of bison

Bison are good runners. But it was their enormous size that best protected them against enemies. Unfortunately, their size did not deter the bisons' human enemies, who killed them for meat, hides, and just for the sport of it. Bringing down a one-ton, seven-foot-high animal with a single shot was exciting for many people. And a creature that large made an easy target.

The Native Americans who roamed the prairie depended on bison for food. They also made clothing and tepees from the bisons' hides and tools from their bones. The U.S. Army knew this and tried to defeat the Indians by killing off the bison. Estimates of the bison population before 1870 range from 30 to 70 million. By 1900 fewer than 600 bison remained in the United States. The public was shocked when it realized that this great symbol of the American West was nearly gone. Both the government and private individuals quickly took steps to restore the bison. They now number about 65,000 in the United States.

A male pronghorn

Another prairie animal often found in groups is the pronghorn. Weighing in at 90 to 120 pounds (41–54 kg) and standing no more than 3 feet (.9 m) high at the shoulder, pronghorn are much smaller than bison. They are sometimes called pronghorn antelope, although they are not related to the true antelope in Africa.

Still, like the antelope of the African plains, pronghorn are built for a grassland existence. Their large eyes see as much detail as those of a human using high-power binoculars. They can run long distances at 40 miles per hour (64 kph), and, if necessary, hit 60 mph (96 kph) for short stretches. Even a one-week-old pronghorn fawn can sprint at 25 miles per hour (40 kph).

Like the bison, pronghorn were hunted nearly out of existence. Their tasty meat was in demand and the mounted head of a big male made an impressive trophy. In less than a century, their numbers dropped from a high of between 30 and 100 million to about 10,000.

Ranchers also shot pronghorn because they thought the animals were eating grass needed by their cattle. Ironically, though, the pronghorn's favorite food is sagebrush, which cattle don't even like to eat.

As they did with the bison, conservationists helped the pronghorn make a comeback. Their population now stands at about 750,000—enough to allow limited hunting. In fact, a tax on hunting rifles and ammunition provided funds to help restore the pronghorn.

Today, the main obstacle to the pronghorn's survival isn't hunting but fences. Like many large grazing animals, pronghorn travel across vast areas of land. Barbed wire fences have cut them off from most of the places where they used to wander and find food.

BARBED WIRE

Farmers have always been bothered by livestock and other animals trampling their crops and have tried to find ways to keep unwanted animals off their land. Stone and wood made convenient fencing materials in Europe and eastern North America. But on the High Plains, such things were expensive and difficult to come by. Farmers tried planting hedge fences of Osage orange and other plants. But these shaded the plants they were protecting and required constant attention. And it took three to five years for a hedge to grow, during which time it could easily be consumed by fire or animals. Smooth wire offered a promising alternative, but cattle and pigs had little trouble getting through it. Then people realized that if tiny, pointed barbs were attached to the wire, the animals would learn to avoid it. This turned out to be an effective way to protect crops, and barbed wire soon helped bring white settlers to the Great Plains, just as the plow had brought them to the tallgrass prairie.

Sandhill cranes above the Platte River in Nebraska

Migratory birds, such as ducks and geese, are temporary residents of the prairie. They use freshwater ponds and marshes called **potholes** to raise their young. Unfortunately, many potholes have been filled in by farmers who want more land to grow their crops. As a result, the number of ducks in North America has steadily decreased.

Countless waterfowl also depend on prairie rivers. Most of the North American sandhill crane population uses the Platte River in southern Nebraska. Each March, half a million of these long-legged wading birds converge on the river before heading north. The sound of their strange calls at sunrise and sunset is one of the most thrilling experiences the natural world has to offer. Some people predict that sections of the Platte River where migrant birds rest may dry up if plans are carried out to build dams upstream. This is yet another example of the way humans change the life of the prairie.

Cattle are now the most common animals on the plains. But they are very different from the native grass eaters. Their digestive systems are less efficient than those of bison. This means that if a bison eats a hundred pounds of grass it will gain more weight than a cow that eats the same amount. In other words, a cow eats a greater quantity of grass relative to its weight than a bison does.

Compared to bison, cattle have a very different effect on the appearance of the prairie. After bison ate most of the plants on a section of land, they would move on to greener pastures. The plants on the overgrazed section could then recover. But cattle don't roam freely across the prairie as bison did; they live on a specific portion of the land. After cattle eat most of their food plants, they may not have anywhere else to go. Unless they are fed hay or moved to another pasture, they will eat each new leaf that appears on the plants in their area. And without leaves, the plants soon die off.

Some native plants, such as big bluestem, decline more quickly than others as a result of heavy grazing. These plants are called **decreasers**. Other native plants, like buffalo grass, are **increasers**. They actually increase with heavy grazing as the decreasers die off.

When a large herd of bison passed through an area, the relative abundance of the increasers rose, while that of the decreasers fell. When the bison moved on, the cycle often reversed itself.

Increasers and decreasers may be grasses, forbs or even bushes like sagebrush. The exact kind of increaser and decreaser plants

Cattle have grazed heavily on this section of shortgrass prairie in Colorado. Sagebrush, an increaser, is thriving as a result.

varies somewhat between the tallgrass, shortgrass, and mixed prairies. All increasers and decreasers are **perennial** plants, that is, they come up year after year from the same roots.

When grazing is very intense, even the increasers may not last. Then a group of grasses and wildflowers called **invaders** moves in to the area. If grazing is very heavy, bare spots on the soil may develop where the increasers and decreasers used to be. If the soil is moist, these bare spots are excellent places for invaders to take root.

Unlike the perennial increasers and decreasers, invaders are annuals, which means they grow from seeds, flower, and die all in one year. Increasers and decreasers generally provide better food for animals than invaders. They contain more nutrition, and their seeds and leaves have fewer sharp points that injure animals' mouths.

A dust storm near Roswell, New Mexico

During the great drought that plagued the prairie states in the 1930s, wells dried up and crops shriveled. At the same time, so many cattle and sheep had grazed on the land's protective cover of sod that it was completely eaten away in some places. As a result, many acres of raw soil were exposed to the prairie winds. As the wind stripped the topsoil, billowing masses of dust darkened the sky. Our central plains soon became known as "the Dust Bowl."

Even today, large clouds of topsoil frequently blow across the Great Plains. When the topsoil is gone, prairie grasses and crops cannot grow in the soil that remains because it is low in nutrients.

Droughts and topsoil loss are just two of the reasons that many people have found it hard to live on the Great Plains. Plains residents must also deal with terribly hot summers, bitterly cold winters, and occasional plagues of locusts. Towns, ranches, and farms are often so far apart that medical help during an emergency may not arrive in time. And the money paid for the products of the plains, such as beef and wheat, isn't always enough for the ranchers and farmers to make a living. Even the discovery of valuable oil and minerals on the plains has produced few lasting benefits. The economy of the Great Plains has always alternated between times of great prosperity and tougher economic times.

Cowboys have a harder time making a living on the prairie than they once did.

Farms in the Midwest may someday be replaced by native prairie.

Currently the plains economy is in a bust, a bad period, which many people fear may not end. Farms and ranches are going out of business so quickly that agriculture may someday disappear from this part of the West. If that happens, the native grasses might return to their original abundance. Former ranch sites that have not been severely overgrazed could change back to a natural state in as little as 20 years. The land might then be as it was when Native Americans hunted bison. Indeed, bison could be reintroduced to large areas of the plains. Some are already calling such an area "the Buffalo Commons."

Large portions of the mixed prairie are already preserved in parks and wildlife refuges. As for the tallgrass prairie, nearly all of it has been plowed under and replaced with crops. Finding a stand of natural tall grass along a roadside or in a forgotten cemetery is as unusual as seeing a grizzly bear or a bald eagle. In fact, tallgrass is so rare that in Elgin, Illinois, two acres of virgin prairie were carefully dug up and transplanted, topsoil and all, to a nature preserve six miles away. The original site became a gravel pit.

Sunflowers on a mixed prairie refuge in Nebraska

Some people love the prairie so much that they collect seeds from tall grasses and forbs for planting elsewhere. More and more institution grounds, roadsides, and neighborhood yards are being planted in big bluestem and other prairie plants. Compared to lawns, native grasses offer many advantages. They need little maintenance, they provide a natural environment for animals, and they are always beautiful, especially in the wind.

With luck, a restored tallgrass prairie may resemble the original in 200 or 300 years. But it may never have the same number and variety of plants and animals that the early pioneers found there.

Only small scraps of virgin tallgrass prairie remain. But even these are important to scientists who have questions about prairie plants. How do these plants endure drought? Do they contain chemicals that might cure human diseases? Some scientists are studying prairie grasses to see if they can be used for human food. Others just want to learn more about what the tallgrass prairie is—what makes it healthy and what does it harm.

Indian paintbrush amid the tall grasses on a Missouri prairie preserve

There is another reason to preserve the prairie. It's part of our heritage as Americans. If given the choice, surely the men and women who first crossed the prairie would want us to save at least some of the land that played such an important part in their lives.

Even though most of our wild prairie has been converted to agriculture, one thing about the prairie still hasn't changed— the beautiful view of the sky. From horizon to horizon, you can still see the ever-changing atmosphere of our earth. Rainbows, lightning, and even tornadoes are visible from many miles away. And on a clear evening, the sun looks so big, it doesn't seem real.

GLOSSARY

adapted: adjusted or changed in order to fit into an environment

decreasers: plants that die off quickly as a result of heavy grazing

drought: a prolonged period when little or no rain falls

evaporation: the process by which water leaves a surface and becomes vapor

forbs: nonwoody plants other than grasses

glaciers: huge sheets of ice

increasers: plants that grow more rapidly as a result of heavy grazing

invaders: plants that thrive where both increasers and decreasers have died as a result of especially heavy grazing

irrigation: bringing water to dry areas to aid crop growth

mollisols: soft, nutrient-rich soils

pollen: the substance produced by flowers that contains male sperm cells

pollination: the process by which pollen is brought to flowers, enabling them to reproduce

pothole: a round, sunken area in the ground that is filled with water

predators: animals that destroy or kill and eat other animals

prevailing winds: winds from the most common direction in a given area. In North America, the prevailing winds are from the west.

rain shadow: an area where rainfall is low, located on the side of a mountain that faces away from the wind

sod: a dense mixture of soil and plant roots

INDEX

ABOUT THE AUTHOR

Frank Staub is the author of several books for children and dozens of magazine articles, film-strips, and slide sets. He holds degrees in Biology and Zoology. He works as a free-lance writer and photographer, which allows him to travel and study the places and events that interest him most. When he's not working, he climbs mountains and enjoys sea kayaking, bicycling, and skin diving.